EWING, P.

P9-CJK-028

SPORTS GREAT PATRICK EWING

—Sports Great Books—

Sports Great Charles Barkley (ISBN 0-89490-386-1)

Sports Great Larry Bird (ISBN 0-89490-368-3)

Sports Great Roger Clemens (ISBN 0-89490-284-9)

Sports Great John Elway (ISBN 0-89490-282-2)

Sports Great Patrick Ewing (ISBN 0-89490-369-1)

Sports Great Bo Jackson (ISBN 0-89490-281-4)

Sports Great Magic Johnson (Revised and Expanded)
(ISBN 0-89490-348-9)

Sports Great Michael Jordan (ISBN 0-89490-370-5)

Sports Great Joe Montana (ISBN 0-89490-371-3)

Sports Great Hakeem Olajuwon (ISBN 0-89490-372-1)

Sports Great David Robinson (ISBN 0-89490-373-X)

Sports Great Darryl Strawberry (ISBN 0-89490-291-1)

Sports Great Isiah Thomas (ISBN 0-89490-374-8)

Sports Great Herschel Walker (ISBN 0-89490-207-5)

SPORTS GREAT
PATRICK
EWING

Jack Kavanagh

—Sports Great Books—

ENSLOW PUBLISHERS, INC.

Bloy St.& Ramsey Ave.   P.O. Box 38
Box 777   Aldershot
Hillside, N.J. 07205   Hants GU12 6BP
U.S.A.   U.K.

Library of Congress Cataloging-in-Publication Data

Kavanagh, Jack.
    Sports great Patrick Ewing / Jack Kavanagh.
        p. cm. — (Sports great books)
    Includes index.
    Summary: Describes the life and career of the noted New York
Knicks basketball player, from his childhood to the present.
    ISBN 0-89490-369-1
    1. Ewing, Patrick Aloysius, 1962–   —Juvenile literature.
2. Basketball players—United States—Biography—Juvenile
literature. 3. New York Knickerbockers (Basketball team)—Juvenile
literature. [1. Ewing, Patrick Aloysius, 1962–   . 2. Basketball
players. 3. Blacks—Jamaica—Biography.] I. Title. II. Series.
GV884.E9K38   1992
796.323'092—dc20
[B]
                              91-41531
                                CIP
                                AC

Photo Credits: Bob Breidenbach

Cover Photo: Bob Breidenbach

Contents

Chapter 1

Sometimes it seems that some grownups still believe in Santa Claus—especially if they happen to be sports fans. They expect their favorite team will win every game. Even if their team is not as good as the other team, it might get lucky. Hope ran high among the fans of the New York Knickerbockers when the 1985 season began. The team had a new superstar, Patrick Ewing. He had been the "College Player of the Year." The Knicks made him their Number One choice in the National Basketball Association draft. The 7-foot tall, 240-pound giant center was counted on to lead the way back to the championship seasons of the past. However, as the Knicks 1985–86 season went along, the team seemed even worse than before.

No one really blamed Patrick Ewing. He impressed everyone with his hustle. In college, at Georgetown University, he had been a team player. He still was. Basketball is a team game, and a single player cannot win games by himself. He needs help. Patrick had joined a team that was in trouble. He was the Knicks' first rookie in many years who was a high draft pick. The way professional teams become better is to choose the best players coming out of college. The teams with the worst records get to pick first. However, a team can also trade its future draft picks for veteran players. A team might think that adding an experienced player to the lineup is more important than waiting for young players to develop. The Knicks had done this in the past, and it had been a mistake.

Even worse, the best player they had, Bernard King, was out for the season. He had been the team's superstar but had injured his knee. Another one of their best players, Bill Cartwright, had played only two games before dropping out of the lineup for the season. Even taller than Patrick at 7 feet 2 inches, Cartwright was expected to join with him to form the "Twin Towers." Without a teammate to share the rebounding, Patrick was double- and triple-teamed. The Knicks were an early season disappointment, and things did not improve. Almost winless on the road, the Knicks were deep in last place in December.

On Christmas Day 1985, thousands of basketball fans jammed Madison Square Garden in midtown New York to see the Knicks' annual holiday game. Regardless of how the season was going, this was a special occasion. Many of the Knicks' fans hoped that Santa Claus would fill their stockings with a surprise gift. If their team could just beat its traditional rival, the Boston Celtics, it would be a real holiday treat.

Any special Christmas prize for the Knicks would be unwrapped before a national television audience. Most people had turned on their sets to watch Larry Bird, the great Celtics' forward. He was on his way to winning his third Most Valuable Player trophy in a row. The Celtics were headed for their second NBA title in the past three years. Already they

Patrick Ewing makes a fast break past his opponent.

were on top of the Eastern Division while the Knicks were at the bottom.

The game started out as just another rout of the Knickerbockers. There were 17,480 fans in the Garden for the opening tap. By the end of the first half, the Knicks were trailing, 45–32. Some people began to leave. Those who remained watched the second half begin as badly as the first one had ended. Midway through the third quarter, the Knicks were down by 25 points. Then, after a time-out, Patrick's teammates gathered around Coach Hubie Brown. They pledged to make an all-out effort. The Knicks started ripping the wrapping off their Christmas present for their fans.

Patrick Ewing took charge of the game—personally. He raged up and down the court. He destroyed the Celtics' front

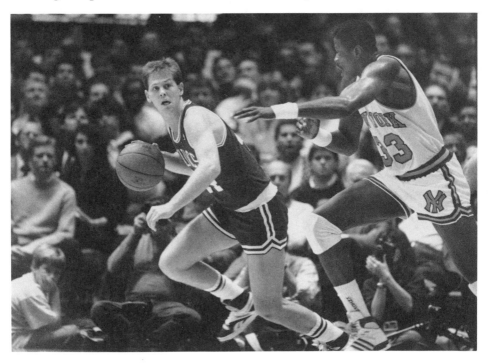

Patrick keeps pace with Danny Ainge of the rival Celtics.

10

line of Robert Parish, Kevin McHale, and Larry Bird. He tossed in turnaround jumpers from far out. He popped in others from close in. Patrick blocked shots, grabbed rebounds, hit open men with bulletlike passes. The Celtics 25-point lead melted away before the fire of Ewing's play. It dropped to 13 points, then 2, and disappeared as the time clock ran out. Patrick had scored 18 points in the fourth quarter, 12 of them in a row. He had almost stolen the game from the Celtics. With only seconds to play, Patrick stripped the ball from Kevin McHale. He whipped it to his teammate Pat Cummings, but a 19-foot shot missed, and the game went to overtime.

Overtime went badly for the Knicks. Patrick, who had limped on a painful knee during the wild second half, dove for a loose ball. He had to be helped to the bench. With their star out of the game, the Knicks gave way to the Celtics and soon trailed, 97–92 with only 1:09 left to play. Then Patrick Ewing got back into the game. He drove past Robert Parish and laid the ball in the net. The Knicks were down by three points. When Ewing hauled down Larry Bird's missed shot from the baseline, the Knicks called time out. Coach Hubie Brown sent in Trent Tucker, his best three-point shooter.

The in-bounds pass went to Patrick Ewing. He shook off Dennis Johnson's attempt to steal the ball and dribbled clear. He found Tucker in the open and passed him the ball. Tucker's shot spun high toward the basket. With eleven ticks left on the time clock, the ball dropped in. The Knicks had carried the Celtics to a second overtime.

This time the Celtics just caved in. With the holiday crowd roaring its approval, the Knicks outscored their Boston rival 16 to 7 for a final score of 113–104. Patrick Ewing had scored a career-high 32 points. The noisy fans filed out of Madison Square Garden. Yes, there was a Santa Claus.

During the Christmas game, Patrick kept the Celtics' powerful front line from scoring.

However, Santa went back to the North Pole. He had delivered a Christmas gift, but nothing more. While the players celebrated in the locker room, Patrick Ewing put more ice on his knee. The next day it was too swollen for him to travel to Chicago for the Knicks' next game. Over the following weeks, Patrick was in and out of the lineup. When he could play, he dominated games and showed he deserved to be voted Rookie of the Year. He won that honor, although he played in only 50 of the 82 games on the Knickerbockers' schedule.

Once again the New York Knicks finished far behind the teams that qualified for the NBA playoffs. Not even Patrick Ewing could change the Knicks into a winner. It would take longer than one season for even a player like Patrick Ewing to help the Knicks gain the playoffs.

Ewing and Denis Johnson of the Celtics scramble to pick up the loose ball.

Chapter 2

Patrick Ewing never saw a basketball until he was twelve years old. When he did, he was a new kid in the neighborhood. He watched other boys playing a strange game in a schoolyard in Cambridge, Massachusetts. It was a long way from Jamaica, the sunny Caribbean island where he had been born.

Patrick's father, Carl, was a mechanic. He worked hard, but jobs were scarce in Trench Town, the ghetto area outside Kingston where the Ewing family lived. Patrick, born on August 5, 1962, was the fifth of seven children. His mother had gone to the United States where she got a job at Massachusetts General Hospital and found a small house for her family. One or two at a time the rest of the family left for the United States. Patrick joined the family in Cambridge on January 11, 1975.

A gangly kid with long arms and legs, Patrick was already six feet tall. He quickly saw that the idea of the game the neighborhood boys were playing was to throw the ball through the hoop. In soccer, the ball had been kicked into a net. Patrick had played goalie back in Jamaica. It was his job to keep the other team from scoring goals. Perhaps this was why defensive play became Patrick's first specialty when he took up basketball. He was already tall enough to leap up and knock the other team's shots away. In soccer, the goalie does not get to score points against the other team. He only defends his team's goal. Patrick was happy to discover that basketball let him do both. He could not only keep the other team from scoring points, but he could also score points himself. He discovered he had a good shooter's eye. He was also taller than most of the other boys and could score easy baskets on tap-ins.

There was something else Patrick brought from the playing fields of his native Jamaica—team pride. To Patrick, a team victory was much more important than personal stats. When he played at the Rindge and Latin High School in Cambridge, Massachusetts, Patrick had both. He became the best high school player in the nation, according to Red Auerbach, the general manager of the Boston Celtics. His high school team won the Massachusetts State Championship in each of Patrick's three varsity seasons. Patrick was the only high school player invited to try out for the 1980 United States Olympic basketball team. He did not make the team, but the experience showed him what to expect when he began playing college ball.

Patrick was lucky to have a caring high school coach, Mike Jarvis. Many top basketball prospects are hounded by college recruiters who want them to play at their schools. It spoils the fun of the player's last year in high school. All too often it results in a player's making a bad mistake in choosing his college. Coach Jarvis talked with Patrick's parents, and all agreed basketball would be only a means of getting a good education. Two of his sisters were already college graduates.

The family knew it was also important that Patrick enjoy college life away from the basketball court.

Colleges knew about Patrick Ewing. There had been a feature story about him in *Sports Illustrated.* An article in *The New York Times* told how his coach had helped Patrick decide where he wanted to go to college. Coach Jarvis had written letters to 150 Division 1 schools. He set the rules. Patrick had lived in this country for only six years. His school, the Rindge and Latin High School in Cambridge, home of Harvard and MIT, had high academic standards. To meet them, Patrick had gone to summer school. He attended the Achievement School, a remedial center for junior high school students in Cambridge.

John Thompson, coach of the Georgetown Hoyas, protected his team from the press. His school's offer was the most attractive to Ewing's parents.

"Pat is quite motivated to do well and is conscientious in getting his work done," Jarvis said in his letter. "He learns a great deal through listening." In order for Pat to be successful in regular college courses, Coach Jarvis said he would need daily tutoring and constant guidance and supervision.

The National Collegiate Athletic Association regulations allow a scholarship candidate to visit up to six schools. All the schools that Patrick checked out met the standard the Ewings had set: Boston College, Boston University, UCLA, North Carolina, Georgetown, and Villanova. If either Boston College or Boston University were selected, Patrick could play close to home. Coach Jarvis's plan was to choose Patrick's college as soon as a sound decision could be made. John Thompson, head coach at Georgetown University in Washington, D.C., made the best impression on Patrick and his parents. Almost as tall as Patrick, he had been a 6-foot, 10-inch center for the Boston Celtics for three seasons. He had backed up the immortal Bill Russell, the player to whom Patrick was being favorably compared. Georgetown was a highly respected university. Most important of all, Coach Thompson had the reputation of graduating his players. They were mostly African American kids from city schools. Like Patrick, they needed the help of faculty advisers. Only a few would make good in professional basketball. Some would become high school coaches. But most would look for jobs after graduation where it did not matter that you had been a hot-shot athlete. Therefore, Georgetown was finally selected.

There was something else about playing basketball for John Thompson. He protected his players from the press. Patrick Ewing was already famous when he came to Georgetown. Coach Thompson ruled out interviews. Too many young players had been made to look foolish or to

Patrick's superior skill on the court brought him to the attention of NBA teams even before he was ready to graduate.

sound dumb by reporters. The Georgetown Hoyas were a close-knit group. They did not shake hands with their opponents. They did high fives among themselves when they beat the other team. Outsiders did not know that the biggest Hoya player, Patrick Ewing, had a warm, friendly personality off the court. Only the basketball floor, he wore a scowl. He was the team's intimidator. He was easily noticed. He had started wearing a T-shirt underneath his sleeveless jersey when he played in drafty high school gyms. He wore the extra shirt in college. Only those close to him knew that beneath it beat the heart of a decent young giant.

Patrick Ewing's four years at Georgetown were as typical as a national superstar can enjoy. He lived in a regular student dorm, and not all his close friends were jocks. He hung out with classmates who had interests other than sports. He worked hard to earn a degree in fine arts. Poster design became his specialty. He was good, but when a signed exhibit of his class work was stolen, he suspected the thief was more interested in his autograph than his artwork. Away from the campus, Patrick worked as an intern for United States Senator Robert Dole. He began to date Rita Williams. She was a Howard University student who worked for Senator Bill Bradley, a former basketball superstar with the New York Knicks.

The Georgetown Hoyas had become a college basketball powerhouse under Coach Thompson. They were part of the tough Big East Conference, but so far they had failed to win a national championship. They had never made it to the Final Four of the NCAA post-season tournament. Patrick took them that far in his first year. As a freshman, Patrick Ewing led Georgetown all the way to the final game of the tournament before they lost by one point to the North Carolina Tar Heels, 63–62. North Carolina had been one of the six schools Patrick had considered. If he had gone there, he would have been on the championship team. Georgetown, of course, might not even have made the tournament without Patrick as its center.

After coming up short in 1983, the Hoyas became NCAA champions in 1984. They beat Houston 84–75, and Patrick was voted the Most Outstanding Player of the tournament. He was picked over Houston's great center, Hakeem Olajuwon, who had been chosen the year before. The next year, 1984, was a banner year for Patrick. He was again invited to try out for the United States Olympic basketball team. This time he easily qualified and led the United States to a gold medal victory over Spain. Away from the protective Georgetown campus, Patrick showed more openness. "Coach Bobby Knight [head coach at Indiana and of the Olympic team] and I enjoyed him," said Iowa coach George Raveling, an Olympic assistant. "We had no problems communicating." About Patrick's reputation for not opening up to the press and public, he said, "I think Patrick tends to be a private person."

The year 1984 was also one for making hard decisions. Patrick still had one more year to play college basketball for Georgetown. However, even his coach, John Thompson, advised him to leave school and take the money the pros were offering. The Portland Trail Blazers were fined $250,000, the largest sum in NBA history, for trying to sign Patrick and Olajuwon when they were only juniors. However, Patrick would not break the promise he made to his mother, who had died the year before. Patrick told her he would stay at Georgetown and earn his degree. It was a promise he would keep to the woman who had worked so hard for her family. She was only fifty-five when she had a massive heart attack at her home in Cambridge, Massachusetts.

Another major event for Patrick in 1984 was the birth of Patrick Aloysius Ewing, Jr., on May 21. Sharon Stanford, the mother of Ewing's son, had been his high school sweetheart. Patrick was happy to be a father, but marriage was not on his schedule. Not yet. He had a final year ahead as a senior at Georgetown. In fact, since the Georgetown basketball program was wrapped in silence, it was not known until a year later that Patrick had a son.

Chapter 3

The pressure on Patrick Ewing during his senior year was even greater than it had been before. He had already led the Hoyas to the NCAA championship. He could not improve on that record. He was an All-American and now had to live up to his reputation. His coach, John Thompson, continued to keep the press away from his team, and the stories that appeared about Patrick contained mostly quotes from his friends. It was clear there were two sides to Patrick. The only side the public saw was that of a strong, determined young giant whose aggressive play won him no friends on enemy courts. The Patrick Ewing his friends told about was a person concerned about others and full of jokes. Things others saw as hostile, such as refusing to sign autographs, were misunderstood. Patrick objected to being the only player sought out with these requests. "I'll sign after you've asked my teammates," he would tell people pushing pieces of paper at him to be signed. Often he would put out his own hand and offer it to any fan who approached him. "I'll be glad to shake your hand," he would tell them. "It means a lot more than having me write my name." Patrick guarded his private life but had a wide circle of friends at Georgetown and back in Cambridge.

One place Patrick always found comfortable was the basketball court, both practicing and playing games. In his first three years at Georgetown, Patrick's intimidating defensive play had been the strongest part of his game. As a senior, he continued to dominate at both ends of the court. He would race back and forth, a thundering part of the team's fast breaks. However, he also developed better techniques as a shooter. He displayed a fine turnaround jump shot and, in his final year, added an unstoppable jump hook to his game. His floor play also improved. His assists jumped from less than 30

Despite his image, Patrick Ewing knew how to have a good time with friends.

Ewing slaps away a shot in a game with Loyola University. At Georgetown, Patrick was a dominant force on both ends of the court.

in a season to almost 50. Patrick was giving up the ball more often so his teammates could score points.

Georgetown is a member of the Big East Conference. It had been formed by nine colleges that consistently had outstanding basketball teams. Boston College and Villanova, two of the schools Patrick had considered, belonged to the Big East. Also in the conference were Seton Hall, Syracuse, Pittsburgh, Providence, Connecticut, and St. John's. The Redmen of St. John's were a particularly bitter rival for Georgetown in Patrick's senior year. They had a superstar of their own, Chris Mullin. He was an outstanding guard, and the fact that he was a hometown player from New York City added to his popularity. Also, he was a white player. It should not have mattered, and on the basketball court it did not. However, all during Patrick's carer he had to deal with racism off the court. Signs were used to taunt him. Wherever he played, he was regarded as the Darth Vader of college basketball.

As the defending NCAA champions, the Hoyas of Georgetown were the team everyone wanted to defeat. Yet they lost only twice while winning 35 games. One of the teams that beat Georgetown was St. John's in a regular season game at Madison Square Garden. The Hoyas evened the score on their home court. The teams met twice more, once in the Big East tournament and once in the NCAA tournament. Patrick Ewing led Georgetown to victories both times. It appeared as though Ewing and the Hoyas were headed for a repeat NCAA championship. For the third time in Patrick's college career, he played in the final game of the tournament. It was the right way for the man called "The Warrior" to end his career.

Patrick had been given this nickname by his coach. "I said when he first came to Georgetown that he reminds me of a warrior," Thompson said. "You can see the pride. On the day of a game, he just glows. He works hard. People always say, 'Well, he looks mean.' And they talk about his attitude. Well, attitude has nothing to do with running for 40 minutes."

Any team that can reach the finals of the NCAA tournament must be outstanding. Nonetheless, Villanova's chances of upsetting the great Georgetown team were slim. Man for man, they did not match up well against the Hoyas. The one thing they had going for them was emotion. Where John Thompson was methodical and cool, the Villanova coach, Roland Massimino, was volatile and fiery. In addition, he was a great coach. His players were as disciplined on the court as Rollie Massimino was off it. He would rip off his

John Thompson hugs Patrick, as Georgetown celebrates a victory in the NCAA tournament playoffs.

sports coat and risk technical fouls to shout at the officials. While the coach was stirring up a storm on the bench, his players would methodically carry out the game plan. It would take a nearly perfect game to beat Georgetown. The Wildcats center Ed Pinckney (6 feet, 9 inches), helped by forward Harold Pressley (6 feet, 7 inches), would have to contain the 7-foot Patrick Ewing. Quickness would count.

The NCAA finals were played in Lexington, Kentucky, far from Washington, D.C., home of the Hoyas, or the Philadelphia area where Villanova is located. However, the crowd was solidly behind the underdog Villanova Wildcats. The game was close all the way. Basket by basket the score went back and forth. Georgetown could never make the big run that would put the game out of reach. When the final buzzer sounded, it was the deliriously happy Wildcats who celebrated a low scoring, 66–64 victory.

In a fiction story, Patrick Ewing would have ended his career by scoring the winning basket. In real life, Patrick was called on to show he had the maturity to accept defeat gracefully. He was gracious during the post-game presentation of trophies. The year before he and his teammates had taken winner's trophies away with them. This year they had to settle for the awards given the runner-up team. Patrick stood up and applauded as each of his teammates came forward. When his name was called, he walked out, smiling, and raised a single finger. Later he explained, "We may not have won the ball game but I feel that we're still number one."

Patrick applauded Ed Pinckney, the Villanova center, when he was given the outstanding player award that had been his the year before. That was easier than watching as the Villanova seniors and Coach Massimino accepted the national championship trophy. Patrick's face had clouded over. It was

Patrick having a conference with teammates. With grace, defending champion Georgetown accepted defeat by Villanova in the finals of the 1985 NCAA tournament.

always easier for him to deal with personal setbacks than to have his team lose.

Several trophies are given each year to the best college basketball player. One, the Eastman Kodak award, is voted on by the college coaches. Patrick Ewing held true to form when he accepted the Eastman Kodak award on the eve of the Final Four weekend of the NCAA tournament. Among the questions he sidestepped were ones about playing St. John's in the semifinal game. He also declined to comment on a future pro basketball career or to compare John Thompson with his Olympic coach, Bobby Knight of Indiana.

Another national award, the John Wooden Award, is voted by the sports writers, some of whom seemed to have downgraded Patrick for being uncooperative with the press. John Thompson's "Hoya paranoia" cost Patrick enough votes to make Chris Mullin of St. John's the winner of the writers' trophy. Asked whether he had been upset that Chris Mullin had won the John Wooden Award, Patrick replied, "I wasn't upset. Chris is a fine player. But I don't wish to get into that either."

He did express himself about winning awards. "That's a hard question. I'm a normal human being like anyone else. I'm happy I won the Eastman Kodak award. It shows all the hard work is starting to get recognition."

The next award for Patrick Ewing was the one for which he would get no trophy—only a contract to play professional basketball for more money than his family ever dreamed existed when they left Jamaica to come to the United States. The National Basketball Association's draft of college players is the true test of worth. There is no room for pettiness when the value of an NBA's franchise is on the line. The Number One player in the draft has the strongest argument when it comes to signing a professional contract. Patrick's interests would be handled by ProServ, a Washington, D.C., company that represents athletes. They were Coach Thompson's agents and, as Patrick explained, "The coach has always done all right in the money department."

In 1985, a new way to select players for the NBA was introduced. In the past, teams had been tempted to lose games at the end of a poor season so they could pick first in the draft. To prevent any situation of this type from arising, the league decided that the seven teams with the worst records would take part in a lottery. The team's name would be drawn. The last one pulled would get first pick. There was so much interest that the drawing took place on national television. David Stern, the NBA commissioner, began with seven sealed envelopes. Each contained the logo of an NBA team. One after another they were opened. Golden State was picked first and got seventh choice. The Sacramento Kings were the sixth choice and the Atlanta Hawks the fifth. Then the Seattle SuperSonics got the fourth choice and the Los Angles Clippers the third. It was down to two teams. Only one more envelope would need to be opened. Everyone else would have been eliminated. The commissioner had trouble with the scotch tape that sealed the envelope. Then he got it opened and announced, "The Indiana Pacers." Bedlam broke loose at the table where the New York Knickerbockers' general manager, David DeBusschere, and his staff were sitting.

DeBusschere had once been a great player for the Knicks. He had given up a promising career as a big league pitcher to play pro basketball. He had been part of the Knicks when they were champions and, in recent years, had taken a lot of blame when the team played badly. There was no question as to whom the Knicks would make the Number One choice of the NBA draft. They had even brought a jersey with Patrick Ewing's name on it. They could have picked the local favorite,

Chris Mullin of St. John's. Some people thought they should. But, all other considerations aside, Mullin could only make a good team a better one. Patrick Ewing was a "franchise player." Like other great centers who had been the Number One draft pick, Kareem Abdul-Jabbar and Bill Walton, Ewing could turn a losing team into a contender. That is what the Knicks gambled on.

There was one more honor waiting for Patrick Ewing. It was the one that meant the most. No trophy or big contract went with it. It was a diploma from Georgetown University. It would grant a degree in fine arts to Patrick Aloysius Ewing. Despite the pressure of four years of intensive championship basketball, Patrick made good on his promise to his mother and family. He graduated and on schedule. Asked if he was sorry his mother was not there to see him graduate, he replied, "Don't worry. She is."

May 25, 1985, was a sunny, warm day in Washington, D.C., as the 1,460 members of the graduating class marched to their seats. It was the university's 186th commencement. Two graduates drew the most attention. Patrick could not hide his seven-foot height, even by sitting with the other graduating seniors of the Georgetown basketball team. They, too, were making good on Coach Thompson's promise to the African American kids from city schools. He had told them they would leave college with a degree. The other graduate that people wanted to see was Pearl Bailey. The sixty-seven-year-old recording star and stage performer was also receiving a bachelor of arts degree. She delivered an inspiring speech to her classmates.

Patrick Ewing's career at Georgetown came to a close as his father, his brothers and sisters, and his friends from Cambridge shared in his pleasure. College had been as good as it can be for a young man whose skills as an athlete make him a celebrity. He had picked Georgetown because he wanted to do more than spend four years in a gym. Patrick had developed himself as a student, as an artist, and as a person as he had perfected his basketball skills. He was ready to leave the protection of Coach John Thompson. He would have a new coach, Hubie Brown, and the New York Knicks would be his new team.

Chapter 4

With his college years behind him, Patrick set out to enjoy his summer. A highlight of Patrick's summer was a visit to his former home in Jamaica. As the airplane dropped down over the waters of Montego Bay, Patrick looked down and said, "Now that's real water down there." Then he laughed and said in a Jamaican accent he had lost long ago, "Ya, mon. Ree-eel wa-taah." It had been more than ten years since Patrick, now a naturalized United States citizen, had left the Caribbean island. He and his father, Carl Ewing, were welcomed by family and friends and saw places they remembered well. Then Patrick flew away again. He was eager to start life in the NBA.

He left the details of his contract in the hands of his agent, David Falk of ProServ. The agency had done well by Michael Jordan and other NBA players. Patrick was sure they would get him a good contract, too. It turned out that way. Patrick Ewing ended up with a $31 million contract that would keep him with the Knicks for ten years.

Patrick Ewing's value to the New York Knickerbockers was already being felt. In June, when the actual draft process took place, 4,000 fans attended the formal drawing at Madison Square Garden's Felt Forum. They cheered when Patrick was officially named by the Knicks and cheered as he held up a white jersey with Number 33 on the back. On the power of the promise of Patrick Ewing, 6,000 season tickets were sold before summer ended. The fans forgot about the past and expected a golden future. "The Warrior" had become "The Savior."

Patrick Ewing played his first game for the Knicks in a preseason exhibition on October 4. Many Georgetown students and fans came to the game against the Washington Bullets. Right away, Patrick was tested. He and Tony Costner, a 255-pound rookie, traded elbows, and Ewing was dwarfed by Manute Bol, another Bullets rookie. Bol was 7 feet, 7 inches tall. Patrick learned about life in pro basketball the hard way. He played against big, heavy men who physically challenged him. The game was faster; no zone defenses were allowed. He would have to learn to pace himself.

Two days later Patrick was thrown out of a game with Atlanta. He had lost his cool, and it cost him $250 to learn that arguing with officials can be expensive. Things went badly during the preseason games. The Knicks finally won a game, but Patrick lost a fight. Although they downed the Indiana Pacers, 121–109, Patrick was thrown to the floor by Steve Stipanovich, also a rookie center. Patrick suffered a bruised elbow, which bothered him all through the season. Looking back at the preseason, he admitted he was intense and aggressive and was being tested. "We were banging, which is part of the game. And he just came out and grabbed me, flung me to the ground and bent my elbow back. Naturally I was

Ewing slaps away a tipoff. Though he was an excellent center, Patrick would be facing bigger and taller centers in the pros.

angry. I'm blamed for everything that happens. I guess that's life," Patrick concluded.

Patrick Ewing played his first NBA regular season game before a sellout Madison Square Garden crowd of 19,591. On October 26, the Knicks opened against the tough Philadelphia 76ers and lost 99–89. The Sixers were led by thirty-year-old Moses Malone, a hardened eight-time All-Star center. Moses had been the league's MVP three times and did a job on Ewing. He outscored Patrick 35 points to 18 and out-rebounded him 13 to 6. However, the veteran sized up the newcomer by saying: "Ewing's a very smart player. He plays the game the way it should be played. He'll be a great player someday."

The Knicks lost their first six games and were 8–19, the worst record in the NBA late in December. Ewing's elbow still bothered him, and his knees were buckling under the pounding. He had to sit out practice sessions to save his legs. As a result, he lacked stamina in the closing minutes of games. Already he had played in eight preseason games and 25 of the 27 regular season games—as many as in a full college season. And the games were longer. Patrick averaged 36.4 minutes per game, almost the top in the league. He was the Knicks' leader with 19.2 points and played his typical defensive game. But, despite his efforts, Patrick had already played in as many losing games as he had in four years at Georgetown.

Looking back at his first three months as a pro basketball player, Patrick said, "I get away from it all everytime I go home at night." He said that during the ride to his home across the Hudson River in New Jersey, he thinks about the game just played. He thinks about what he did and what he failed to do. While at Georgetown he had enjoyed painting, but so far this season, "I just haven't had the time. I'm still getting adjusted to the lifestyle, all the traveling."

Faster than college games, pro games demanded a lot of running. Like Patrick Ewing, many players suffer numerous knee problems as a result.

Then came the Christmas Day game with the Boston Celtics when Patrick and the Knicks surprised their fans with the famous double-overtime win. However, it was to be only a glimpse of what might have been and someday would be again. Patrick Ewing was not an instant fix for an ailing franchise. Still, the *Christian Science Monitor* quoted an NBA scout who reported: "Patrick Ewing is two things: the best rookie in the league this season and also the most valuable rookie. There is a difference, because some guys with exceptional talent just play for themselves." Patrick was impressing the NBA with his teamwork as well as his individual ability.

The coaches of the league recognized Patrick Ewing's stature by naming him to the All-Star game. This is an honor hardly ever given to a rookie. Even though the Knicks were 18–32 at the All-Star break, Ewing's play had been outstanding. However, on February 6, four nights before the All-Star game, Patrick injured his right knee in a game with the Utah Jazz. It was to prove a serious injury and was too painful to allow him to play in the All-Star game. He also sat out the next seven games. When he returned to action, he was averaging 21.2 points and 9.3 rebounds for an understaffed team. He had been named the rookie of the month for November and January.

On March 11 it was announced that Patrick Ewing needed arthroscopic surgery on his right knee. He had played just four games after returning to the lineup. Then, leaping to block a shot in a game on March 6 at Washington, he had re-injured his ailing knee. On the morning of March 15, Patrick entered Lenox Hill Hospital in New York City. The surgery on his knee took only thirty minutes, and Patrick was sent home that afternoon. Patrick was told to spend the summer months swimming and biking to make his knee strong again. He could

Ewing watches from the bench. Due to his knee injuries, Patrick sat out the end of the 1985-86 season.

shoot baskets, but he could not run until the Knicks training camp opened in the fall.

Patrick's debut season was over. He had played in 50 of New York's 82 scheduled games. He had given his best effort and proved he belonged in the National Basketball Association. On May 19, the basketball writers named Patrick Ewing the "Rookie of the Year." He was an easy winner with 36 votes. Xavier McDaniel of the Seattle SuperSonics and Karl Malone of the Utah Jazz finished far behind.

Patrick accepted the award with a gracious speech. "It was very hard to watch your teammates and not be able to play," he said. "I'm honored to receive this prestigious award. Hopefully next year there'll be a championship trophy, too."

Chapter 5

The New York Knicks fans hoped Patrick Ewing was right when he talked about a championship season. He had spent the summer back at Georgetown. He made his knee strong again by swimming and biking. He took a course in handling money now that he was making so much of it. Patrick, Jr., stayed with him, and they went to the zoo and did things little boys like to do with their fathers. Then it was time to report to the Knicks' training camp.

Patrick's knee was sound again. The team's great backcourt star, Bernard King, was still unable to play, but Bill Cartwright, who had been in only two games during Patrick's rookie year, was ready. Coach Hubie Brown then began to use Cartwright and Ewing in the lineup together. He called it a "Twin Tower" offense. The problem was that both Cartwright and Ewing were centers. Coach Hubie Brown used the faster Patrick Ewing as a power forward. Out of position, Patrick's game suffered. The Knicks began as poorly as they had ended last season. By Christmas they were 7–21. They had lost 12 of their first 16 games and the coach was fired. Bob Hill, the assistant coach, took over. He put Patrick back at center, his natural position.

Patrick Ewing had learned from his rookie season that he could not expect to play at full speed throughout every game. Perhaps the biggest change was in Patrick himself. He relaxed and talked to reporters about how much different things were. "I'm a year older and a year wiser," he said. "I'm still basically a private person, and I don't go out a lot. When I'm home, there's not going to be a headline the next morning saying Patrick Ewing was out making a fool of himself last night."

Patrick might have learned to avoid trouble off the court, but he still got into it during games. On December 16, in a game with the Celtics, he tangled with Boston's backup center, Greg Kite. Patrick was fined $3,000 for his part in the fight. The season was not going well. Then, just as had happened last year, the Knicks fans got a Christmas Day surprise. Actually, many fathers had taken their sons to Madison Square Garden to see a visiting player, Michael Jordan. The high-scoring forward of the Chicago Bulls was a crowd pleaser. While Patrick wore a determined scowl, Michael played with an easy-going smile. On Christmas Day Michael Jordan delivered what people had come to see. He scored 30 points and made spectacular baskets. However, this was below his league-leading average of 37.4 points, and he scored only 4 points in the final quarter and none in the final five minutes. The climax of the game belonged to Patrick Ewing. He had learned to save his best efforts for when baskets counted the most—at the finish.

The Knicks and Bulls came into the last half minute of the game tied. Then, on a give-and-go pass from Patrick Ewing, guard Gerald Henderson banked in a basket for an 84–82 lead. Everyone looked to Michael Jordan to tie the game or shoot a long-range bomb to go ahead. He had three men covering him, yet he put up a double-pump jumper. The shot missed, but Dave Corzine of the Bulls grabbed the rebound and put it in. Tie score. Corzine had been fouled and turned it into a three-point play. The Bulls led, 85–84. Time for one last play by the Knicks. It was not Patrick who took what seemed to be the final shot. He set a screen for Trent Tucker, who sent a 20-foot jumper toward the basket. It missed. Patrick was blocked out by Michael Jordan, but the ball bounced off Jordan's hands. It bounded high in the air and Patrick went up for it. He grabbed the ball and, while still airborne, put up a short jumper that dropped in for the winning basket, 86–85. It sent the Knicks fans home once again believing in Santa Claus.

However, just as had happened the year before, the holiday spirit did not last. Patrick had learned to pace himself better but still made too many foolish fouls. And his temper got away from him again. This time it flared against the Detroit Pistons, and he was called for elbowing their most aggressive player, Bill Laimbeer. The Pistons used the foul shots charged against Patrick to win a game that dropped the Knicks to 16–38. They had no hope to even make the playoffs. More injuries hit the team. Bill Cartwright's foot injury flared again, and Pat Cummings tore a finger ligament.

Patrick, whose scoring average had slipped, began wearing contact lenses, and they helped. The Knicks won four straight games, and Patrick averaged 27 points and shot 61 percent from the floor wearing contacts. Then, the injury the Knicks feared the most happened. With 16 games left to play, Patrick was suddenly done for the season. He slipped on a wet spot and fell. This time it was his left knee that gave way. Patrick was given a knee brace to wear and told to rest up for the next season.

Patrick's temper has often gotten him into fights. This one with Celtic Greg Kite cost him $3,000!

Patrick had played in 63 games, 13 more than in his rookie season. He had missed three games when his knees were too painful for him to play. He left a scoring record of 21.5 points and was ranked sixth in shot blocking. He averaged 8.8 rebounds. He had not been named to the All-Star team and was still short of being "The Savior" of the Knicks' franchise.

When Patrick reported to training camp for his third season with the Knicks, he had a new coach. Rick Pitino had been the college coach of the year the season before. He had taught a group of youngsters at Providence College how to play as a team. They surprised everyone by reaching the Final Four of the NCAA tournament. Coach Pitino taught a running and trapping style of basketball. The other team was pressured aggressively every minute. It might work with enthusiastic college kids, but no one thought that professionals would play that way. Patrick Ewing did, however. He had known Rick Pitino as a young coach at Boston University. Patrick, then an area high school player, would go to the B.U. gym and watch. He had also attended summer basketball camps where Rick Pitino taught.

Pitino said, "I've known Patrick since the ninth grade. He's always been happy-go-lucky. He's fair and polite. And he's attentive; he looks you in the eye and has a great willingness to learn. You tell him something and he does it right away and masters it."

When the 1987–88 season began, Pitino had to set his system in place. He had been an assistant coach to Hubie Brown, Patrick's first NBA coach, but the team's players had changed since them. At first, looking at the league standings, it seemed the Knicks were just as bad as ever. However, they were losing tough games, often in overtime. And they lost games because Rick Pitino's style was hard to learn and play well. He kept telling everyone that the team would gel in the

Ewing concentrates on making a foul shot. His determined will to learn is a great asset, and something many coaches appreciate.

second half of the season. And he kept his fingers crossed hoping that Patrick would not get hurt again.

Christmas came, and the Knicks' fans hopefully hung their stockings at Madison Square Garden. The Detroit Pistons, with Isiah Thomas leading the way, came to New York riding an eight-game winning streak. They led the Central Division of the NBA. The Knicks played hard and led by 14 points midway through the third quarter. Then they let the game get away, making foolish mistakes. The Pistons tied the game with 1:34 to play and won it 91–87. Coach Pitino hoped everyone would be patient. He had a bright rookie, Mark Jackson, in the backcourt. Yet, he knew that in New York the only thing that matters is winning. Pitino hoped the fans would be patient until his team learned to play his style for a full game. He did not want his young prospects traded away.

Patrick Ewing was named to the All-Star game. He was the Knicks' only player on the team. Coming in mid-February, the All-Star game marks the halfway point of the NBA schedule. And, as Rick Pitino had promised, it also was the point where the Knicks began to gel as a team. February became the first winning month for the Knicks since March, 1984. Patrick had not even been on the team back then. The Knicks roared into March with two wins on the road. Until then they had won only one of twelve games away from home. March was a winning month, too. They began to think about making the playoffs. On April 2, they were tied with the Washington Bullets, still at the bottom of the division. However, the Cleveland Cavaliers were only two games ahead of them, and the Philadelphia 76ers, a game and a half. Two of the four teams would reach the playoffs.

The Knicks had won 32 games. This was almost the same team that won only 24 games in each on Patrick's first two seasons. Ewing was averaging 19.3 points and was third in the

Patrick is trapped by surrounding guards. The Knicks tried this same strategy against Michael Jordan.

league in blocked shots. He had not missed a game, although ice packs on his knees were a ritual after every game. He explained, "It's not because my knees hurt, but because my knees are my future. They are my career."

The Knicks played their last home game of the season on April 19. They had edged past the Sixers and Pacers and were tied with the Bullets. Michael Jordan led the Chicago Bulls onto the court to play the Knicks before their eighth sellout crowd of the season. When Jordan led the Bulls back to their dressing room, he had scored 47 points and beaten the Knicks single-handedly. He had been trapped every time he got the ball but still made his baskets. The Knicks made it close, but the 121–118 loss made a playoff spot seem out of reach. They would have to beat the Pacers at Indianapolis. They started badly, missing their first eight shots. Yet, by the half, they trailed by only a point. During half-time they learned the Sixers had lost. If they won this game, they would make the playoffs. If they lost, they would go home.

The second half was played at a breakneck pace. With under two minutes remaining, the score was tied. The Knicks got a basket and held a two-point lead with four seconds to play. The Pacers had the ball. "No threes," Coach Pitino shouted. He expected Patrick's nemesis, Steve Stipanovich, to take the final shot. "Don't let him take a three," he told Ewing. "Leave your feet if you have to, but don't let him take a three."

As expected, the ball was in-bounded to Stipanovich. Patrick rushed him and leaped high. The Pacer sidestepped and began a drive on the basket. He was inside the three-point range. A tie and overtime was the best Stipanovich could hope for now. Then he stumbled and sent a desperation shot toward the basket. It missed, and the Knicks were in the playoffs! The Knicks bench players rushed onto the court, and the shouting

Patrick aggressively guarding Robert Parish of the Celtics.

teammates piled on top of each other. At the bottom was the injured Patrick Ewing.

Now that the Knicks had made the playoffs, they had to take on Larry Bird and the Celtics—in Boston. The Knicks were simply outclassed in the first two games. However, when the playoffs shifted to Madison Square Garden for game three, they were inspired by their cheering home fans. The lead shifted back and forth, and the game was tied, 45–45, at halftime. The Knicks had pressed the Celtics on every play. Bird had only 10 points. The Knicks took a 10-point lead in the final quarter only to have the Celtics come back and tie the game 94–94 with less than two minutes to play. Then Patrick won the game. It was not with booming slam dunks, nor with hook shots or turnaround jumpers, but with foul shots. Two

Without Larry Bird, the Knicks were able to overcome the Celtics in the Atlantic Division of the NBA.

broke the tie, and two more helped build the lead to a final 109–100 score.

Bedlam broke loose, but the cheering stopped the next day. The powerful Celtics eliminated the Knicks from the playoffs. Late in the fourth quarter, the Knicks led, 83–77. Then the Celts made a final run. They pulled even and went ahead to win 102–94. Patrick Ewing had dominated the rebounding. He took down 20 shots off the boards. The Knicks had fought to the final buzzer. Their fans cheered them as they left the court. Coach Pitino had turned the tide, and Patrick Ewing was riding the crest.

Chapter 6

The 1988–89 season was a success in many ways. The Knicks won the Atlantic Division of the Eastern Conference. It was their first divisional title since 1973. They were in the playoffs. Only the Detroit Pistons and the Cleveland Cavaliers, of the Central Division, had better conference records. Rick Pitino's running and trapping style was now established, and Patrick Ewing was a dominant force in the NBA. On February 4, 1989, Patrick reached the 5,000-point career milestone. He was twice named NBA player of the week. He played in the All-Star game again and made both the second All-NBA team and All Defensive team.

The Knicks had vaulted to the top over the Boston Celtics, who played without Larry Bird almost all season. The team made a specialty of a bombs-away offense. They set a new league record with 386 successful three-point field goals. The Knicks began the playoffs by winning three straight from the Philadelphia 76ers. They were not easy games to win, however. Two were won by one point, and the final went into overtime. It was a big improvement over last year, of course, when the Knicks had managed only one win in the opening round. They next took on the Chicago Bulls in the semifinal round, where the winner had to take four games.

The Chicago Bulls, with Michael Jordan, came to New York. However, in addition to Michael, they now had Bill Cartwright, the Knicks' former center. Cartwright was no longer hobbled by broken bones in his foot. He knew Patrick's moves better than any other center in the league. They had gone head-to-head in hundreds of practice sessions. Although Patrick's stats were better than Cartwright's in the playoff series, his floor play was below standard. The opening game went to overtime with the visitors winning. The Knicks tied the series in New York but were outplayed in the first two games in Chicago. They postponed defeat by pulling out the final game in Chicago, but then they were beaten in a thriller, 113–111, when the teams returned to New York City.

The season over, Patrick Ewing checked into Lenox Hill Hospital again. Once more his right knee needed arthroscopic surgery. Again he went back to Washington to strengthen his knee. He biked and went swimming during the summer. He made a change in his weightlifting program. He wanted to increase his upper body strength. Patrick gave up the use of Nautilus equipment and switched to free weights. His muscular build increased from 240 pounds to 255 pounds. He was told he would become the NBA's best player. His son, Patrick, Jr., again spending the summer with his father, heard this. "My daddy is already the best," the five-year-old boy insisted.

The 1989–90 season began with a new coach for the Knicks. Rick Pitino had decided to go back to college coaching. When an offer came to rebuild the basketball program at the University of Kentucky, he took it. Stu Jackson, the Knicks' assistant coach, moved into the top spot.

Patrick's statistics would be better the way the new coach ran the team. Rick Pitino had liked the three-point play. His shooters popped away from long range. Patrick made most of his baskets from in close.

Patrick began his all-everything season by being the NBA player of the month for November. Not only were his stats rising, but big improvement came in his passing. Patrick was selected All-NBA starting center for the Eastern Conference in the All-Star game. He also became the All-NBA first-team center.

Patrick was a scoring machine during the campaign. He broke the Knicks all-time season scoring record with 2,347 points. The old mark had stood since 1962. He set another club record with 922 field goals. He had a career record of 51 points in a game and set a team record by scoring 20 or more points in 28 consecutive games. His most dominating game as a pro came on November 29 at Golden State. He not only scored 44 points, but he also had a career best with 24 rebounds.

Even though Patrick had his best season ever, the Knicks still failed to win the championship he wanted so much. They slipped from first to third in the Eastern Division. The Boston Celtics, with Larry Bird back in action, won the division and met the Knicks in the first round of the playoffs. The Celtics, who almost never lose at the Boston Garden, won the first two games. Then Patrick got going, and the Knicks won the next three games. He played like a superstar. In the final three games, Patrick scored 108 points and had 140 rebounds and 16 assists.

In the semifinal round against the Detroit Pistons, the defending champions, the Knicks fell behind. As had happened with Boston, New York lost the first two games on the other team's court. Then the teams came to New York to

Part of Ewing's better play in the 1990-91 season involved better passing. Instead of trying to make all the shots, Patrick here looks for an open teammate.

play game three at Madison Square Garden. Patrick rose to the occasion. He had been held to an average of under 20 points in the first two playoff games. In game three he scored 45 points, a career high in the playoffs. He grabbed 13 rebounds and had 6 assists. Patrick Ewing dominated defensively, too. He blocked an Isiah Thomas layup in the closing seconds. Isiah was held to 20 points. Bill Laimbeer had only 18. Patrick spiked the big guns of the Pistons.

However, Patrick Ewing could carry the Knicks no farther—not against the superior Detroit Pistons. After they had eliminated Patrick's team, they went on to repeat as NBA champions. The Pistons defeated the Chicago Bulls, 4 games to 3, in the Eastern Conference finals. In the championship finals they easily defeated the Portland Trail Blazers, winner of the Western Conference, 4 games to 1.

When the season was over, Patrick married Rita Williams. Mrs. Patrick Ewing was now a law student at Georgetown University. The Ewings make their home in Potomac, Maryland, just across the river from Washington, D.C.

As he began his first full season of the 1990s, he talked about his frustrations. The team had another new coach, John MacLeod, but the new players Ewing had hoped for were missing. Patrick was reaching his peak, but many of his teammates were already past their own.

From their high season record of 52-30 in the 1988-89 season, the Knicks fell to 45-37 in 1989-90, and again in the 1990-1991 season to 39-44. Patrick wasn't happy with the way things were going.

Ewing and his agent Dave Checketts decided to pursue a special clause in his contract. The clause said that if Ewing was not among the four highest paid players in the NBA in the 1991-92 season, he would automatically become a restricted free agent. A restricted free agent can accept offers from other teams. The player's current team then has fifteen days to match the new offer.

Hakeem Olajuwon of Houston, Michael Jordan of Chicago, and John Williams of Cleveland all received yearly salaries higher than Ewing, but he was still among the top four. While Larry Bird had a lower yearly salary, a special bonus he received for signing a new contract raised his income for the 1991-92 season above Ewing's. This made Ewing the fifth highest paid player.

So Patrick and his agent took their case to the Knicks. The Knicks management disagreed with Ewing that Bird would be the fourth highest players. So, the case had to be decided by an independent arbitrator. When the arbitrator made his decision, he ruled in favor of the Knicks.

Knicks fans were not pleased with what they saw as Patrick's desire to leave his losing team. All waited anxiously to see what would happen. A settlement was finally reached and Patrick showed up to practice with the Knicks for the 1991-2 season. He seemed eager and happy to be there—a good sign that there were no hard feelings between the two parties.

It was also announced in the fall of 1991 that Patrick Ewing was chosen to be part of the 1992 U.S. Olympic basketball team. This would be the first Olympic basketball team in U.S. history to feature professional athletes. The team would feature the best of the NBA including Michael Jordan, Larry Bird, and Magic Johnson.

Patrick could look back on the last half of the 1980s as the years he developed into a great professional basketball player. He had been the best in college at Georgetown. He was becoming the best in pro basketball. Still, what Patrick Ewing wanted above all else was a team championship.

Patrick going over the top of an opponent. Perhaps one day he would be able to help bring the Knicks an NBA Championship.

"I won in high school," Patrick said, "I won in college, but I can't win in the pros, not yet anyway." Nothing short of a championship ring will satisfy Patrick's idea of winning. He had always played for champions before coming into professional basketball. He is determined he will again.

CAREER STATISTICS

College

Year	Team	GP	FG%	REB	PTS	AVG
1981-82	Georgetown	37	.631	279	469	12.7
1982-83	Georgetown	32	.570	325	565	17.7
1983-84	Georgetown	37	.658	371	608	16.4
1984-85	Georgetown	37	.625	341	542	14.6
	Total	143	.620	1316	2184	15.3

NBA

Year	Team	GP	FG%	REB	AST	STL	BLK	PTS	AVG
1985-86	New York	50	.474	451	102	54	103	998	20.0
1986-87	New York	63	.503	555	104	89	147	1356	21.5
1987-88	New York	82	.555	676	125	104	245	1653	20.2
1988-89	New York	80	.567	740	188	117	281	1815	22.7
1989-90	New York	82	.551	893	182	78	327	2347	28.6
1990-91	New York	81	.514	905	244	80	258	2154	26.6
	Total	438	.531	4220	945	522	1361	10323	23.6

Index